CLICK TRICKS!

10 FUN AND EASY TRICKS ANY DOG CAN LEARN

CLICK TRICKS!

10 FUN AND EASY TRICKS ANY DOG CAN LEARN

BY KAREN PRYOR

FALL RIVER PRESS

Book originally published in 2003 as *Click-A-Trick*

Text © 2003, 2010 by Sunshine Books, Inc.

This 2010 edition published by Fall River Press,
by arrangement with Sunshine Books, Inc.

This book is part of *Click! Tricks*
and is not to be sold separately.

Illustrations by William Cypser

Fall River Press
122 Fifth Avenue
New York, NY 10011

ISBN: 978-1-4351-2368-7

Printed and bound in China

1 3 5 7 9 10 8 6 4 2

Contents

Introduction 6

Quick-Start Guide 8

Here Girl! 11

Sit and Down 14

Gimme Five 18

Fun with a Box 20

Speak! and Shh! 23

Find the Keys 25

Fetch 27

Hide and Seek 30

Shut the Door 33

Say You're Sorry 37

Finding Out More 40

Tricks for Clicks

Once your dog has mastered the basic behavior required to make him a good and safe pet (like coming when called and leash manners), you might want to teach him a few fun tricks that will keep him busy and you and your family or guests amused. This book has ten tricks that are easy to teach using the clicker training method but will wow everyone who sees them performed.

Why teach tricks? Tricks are fun. Tricks show people how smart your great dog can be (and make you look good too!) But there's more to it than that. Learning tricks can actually teach your dog to learn faster, pay more attention to you, and do the "important" things better too.

People sometimes think that tricks are different from serious behaviors, such as "Come Here!" But dogs don't see the difference. If it works for them, they'll do it, whatever it is, and they'll do it willingly, with a happy face and wagging tail. So pull out your clicker and give it a try!

"How did you DO that?"

Instead of leading the dog with food or moving him physically through a new trick, clicker trainers break the end goal down into many small parts. By clicking and reinforcing one little part at a time, you can easily teach tricks that would be next to impossible to train the old-fashioned way. Clicker training is dog trainers' slang for a positive reinforcement training system based on operant conditioning. Instead of punishing the dog when he does something bad, you reward him with a click and a treat when he does something good. The dog will soon associate a click as something good and be able to learn all sorts of behaviors and tricks. If you are not familiar with clicker training, read the Quick Start Guide on page 8 carefully to learn this easy and effective training method.

Each trick in this book is divided into a series of steps. In Step #1, you learn what tiny move to start with, and how to get only that move to happen. When you see the dog make the move, you click, following up with a tiny treat. The click tells the dog what he did that worked, so he immediately wants to make that move again; and again you click and treat.

When you and the dog are both confident that he knows the first step, you raise your goals and start clicking and treating for the next step. As you move through the steps, you will be told when to start using a specific word or gesture that cues the dog to do that trick and no other. When you finish all the steps, your trick will be perfect and your dog will be able to do it any place and any time you ask.

Dogs can be creative!

Did you know that some dogs can think up their own tricks? If your dog suddenly does something new and funny or wonderful, go with it! Click it! Even if you don't have a clicker at the moment, you can make a mouth click and then run and get a tiny treat; clicking is about communication, not just about the food. Even one click can make the dog more likely to do that cute behavior again, giving you another chance to click and treat.

Did you and your dog come up with something new to clicker train? Tell me about it! Just send an email to Karen@clickertraining.com. I love the new, creative trick ideas that come from clicker trainers—and from their oh-so-smart clicker dogs!

Happy clicking,
Karen Pryor

BEFORE YOU START TEACHING YOUR DOG HOW TO "GIMME FIVE," YOU need to know the basics of clicker training. Using a clicker to train an animal is easy as long as you keep the following clicker rules in mind.

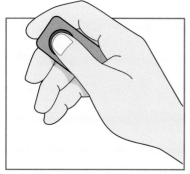

A clicker makes a snapping noise when you press down on the button. This noise will soon become a reinforcer to your pet, letting it know when it has done a positive behavior.

1 To get started, push and release the button on the clicker, making a two-toned click. Then give your dog a treat. The treats should be small and delicious. This will get your dog used to the click sound, and allow him to relate it to something positive.

2 Make sure you click DURING the desired behavior, not after it is completed. The timing of the click is crucial. Give the treat after the click; the timing of the treat is not important.

3 Click when your dog or other pet does something you like. Practice with something easy that the pet is likely to do on its own. (Ideas: sit; come toward you; touch your hand with its nose.)

4 You can fix bad behavior by clicking good behavior. Click a puppy for relieving itself in the proper spot. Click for paws on the ground, not on the visitor. Instead of scolding for barking, click for silence.

5 Keep raising your goal. As soon as you have a good response, start asking for more. Wait until the dog stays down a little longer, comes a little father, sits a little faster. Then click.

6 When your pet is showing you the behavior spontaneously, trying to get you to click, you can begin offering a clue, such as a word or a hand signal. Start clicking for the behavior if it happens during or after the cue. Start ignoring that behavior when the cue wasn't given.

To familiarize Murphy with the clicker, the handler gives him a treat and clicks the clicker at the same time, so Murphy knows the clicker is good, not bad.

7 Don't order your dog around; clicker training is not command-based. If your pet does not respond to a cue, it is not disobeying; it just hasn't learned the cue completely. Try working in a quieter place. If you have more than one pet, separate them for training.

8 If you are not making progress with a particular behavior, you are probably clicking too late. Accurate timing is important.

CLICK!

A) *This is Murphy. He is being taught to turn in a circle. Here, he is just beginning to move to the right. He is clicked for even just starting to head in the right direction.*

B) *As Murphy continues the circle the handler clicks him along the way.*

C) *Murphy has completed the turn because he has learned that turning gets him clicks.*

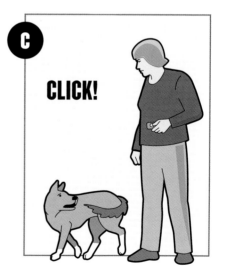

Here Girl!

HAVING YOUR DOG COME WHEN CALLED IS AN IMPORTANT BUT FUN behavior to train. Whether your pet is lost or you just want to show off for friends, learning Here Girl! is a necessity.

1 Grab your clicker, some treats, and your pooch.

2 Sit on the floor and try to coax your dog over to you. When she comes, click and treat. (Don't try to coax the dog with treats. Hide the treats until she's completed each task— then click and treat.)

3 Get up, move, and try again. Click and treat. Repeat several times.

4 Next, call the dog by her name when she is in another room. Try this at unexpected times during the day. Always click and treat when your dog responds. If she doesn't respond, don't give her a second chance. Let your dog see you put away the clicker and treats.

5 Next, try using helpers sitting in different areas of a room. Have your helpers call your dog's name one at a time. When she reaches the helper, you click and the helper treats. This activity can be a lot of fun for children.

A) *Murphy is working on the "Come" command. The leash is used as insurance so he does not run away. It is not used to pull him, or to reel him into position. To begin with, Murphy is clicked and rewarded for being held by the collar.*

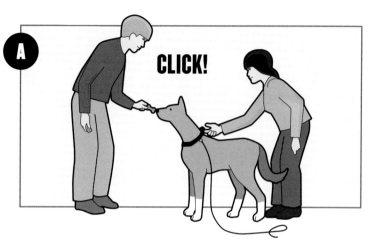

CLICK!

B) *One handler stays with Murphy while the other goes a short distance away. As soon as the second handler calls his name, Murphy is released.*

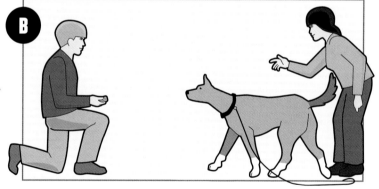

6 Practice calling your dog back and forth between two people outdoors. If your dog loves to bolt, put her on a long leash for safety while you click and treat.

7 If your dog has been ignoring "come" for years, a reliable recall may take weeks to learn. For a puppy, it might just take a couple of days. Be patient. If you find that your dog is not responding at all, try ignoring her. If that fails, put away your clicker, catch the dog and go home. She'll get the message that the fun is over.

8 To maintain the behavior over time, you don't always need to click and treat. Sometimes, if you call to your dog and she responds letting her off the leash to chase squirrels can be a great reward.

CLICK!

C) *Murphy heads for the second handler.*

D) *The moment he reaches the second handler Murphy is clicked and given a treat.*

Sit and Down

ANOTHER BASIC BEHAVIOR, TEACHING YOUR DOG TO SIT AND LIE down is an essential building block for other behaviors. It also goes a long way in getting your dog to calm down or stay in one place.

1 Take some treats in your closed hand and stand in front of your dog.

2 Move the treat across your dog's head between its ears. When he looks up, click and treat. Repeat several times.

3 Now lean over your dog a little so that he leans backward. As soon as his hind legs start to fold, click and treat. Repeat several times.

4 Eventually, your dog will sit. Click and treat. Move away, coax your dog to you, and see if he'll sit on his own. Click and treat. Move again, and repeat. If he sits, click and treat.

5 Now, teach him to stay seated. Let him sit, but wait a few seconds, then click and treat. Repeat several times.

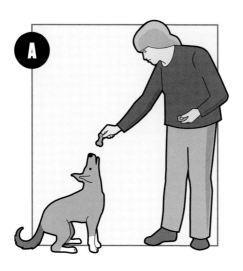

CLICK!

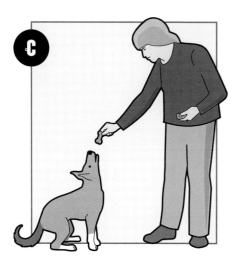

A) *The treat is held above Murphy's head. As he looks up, he will lower his tail-end towards the ground.*

B) *Click! Murphy is clicked as soon as he offers a sit.*

C) *It doesn't matter if Murphy gets up when the food reward is given. It is the click that marks the correct behavior.*

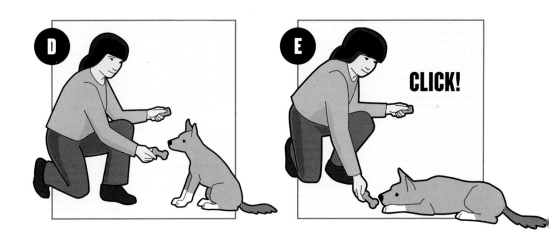

D) *Now that Murphy is sitting reliably, the treat can be used to lure him towards the ground.*

E) *As soon as he goes into the down, he is clicked and rewarded.*

F) *The lure can gradually be withdrawn, and Murphy is clicked for staying in the down position.*

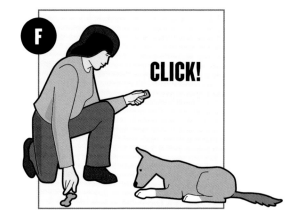

6 Once "sit" is mastered, try "down." As your dog is sitting, put your closed treat hand to his nose. Move it downward between his paws, keeping your hand close to his body. His nose will follow your hand, and he'll start to lie down. Once those front legs bend, click and treat.

7 Try again. If he lies down, click and treat. If not, coax him up and try again.

8 Now, stay still. Wait for him to lie down on his own. Click and treat for any movement in the right direction. Each time let him go a little bit further before you click.

9 Now, add verbal commands for each behavior. Say, "sit" just as he's sitting. Click and treat. Repeat several times.

10 Click and treat only when he responds to "sit." Then add "down" the same way.

TEACH YOUR DOG THIS ADORABLE TRICK EASILY USING THE CLICKER technique. She'll be wowing friends and visitors in no time!

1 Sit down somewhere quiet with a clicker, your dog, and a bunch of small treats.

2 Watch the dog and click the instant her right front paw moves, for any reason. Toss the treat so your dog has to move to get it. Repeat rapidly five times.

A) *Murphy is clicked and given a treat as soon as he slightly moves his paw.*

3 If your dog just sits and looks at you, move a treat back and forth of her nose to lure her into shifting her weight. Click and treat any lift or movement of her right front paw, however tiny. Repeat.

4 When paw movements become more pronounced, click higher movements, at the top of the movement, and stop clicking lower or smaller movements.

5 When her paw lift reaches her shoulder height put your hand in the path of the movement back down. Click at the instant her paw touches your hand. Repeat.

6 Move your hand slightly so your dog must aim for your hand with her paw, to get clicked. Click and treat when your dog slaps her paw against your outstretched hand.

B

7 Click for stronger swats, as you hold your hand higher. Offer hand to the left of her, to the right of her, and while you are standing up. Treat generously for increased efforts.

8 Now, start saying "Gimme five!" when you hold out your hand. Click and treat when she responds.

B) *When Murphy lifts his paw as high as his shoulder height, his owner puts his hand in the path of the movement back down. When Murphy's paw touches his owners' hand, he will get a click and a treat.*

9 Repeat the verbal command and gesture in different locations and times of day.

10 Show off your friendly dog to your friends!

Fun with a Box

THIS IS A GREAT GAME TO PLAY WITH A CAUTIOUS DOG. IT GIVES YOUR dog courage to try and learn new things. It's also great for a naturally curious dog and will allow him to explore.

CLICK!

CLICK!

A) *Murphy is clicked for going near the box.*

B) *Although it may not seem like it, putting his paw on the box is a big step for Murphy to take and he is clicked again.*

1 Take any cardboard box and cut the sides down to about three inches. Put the box on the floor. Keep your clicker and some treats handy.

2 Click and treat every time your dog looks in the box, walks past it, steps towards it, etc. Don't worry about over treating. Get him excited about the box. If he's suspicious, be patient and creative.

3 Once your dog is familiar with it, click and treat for stepping in the box, pushing the box, chewing the box, or anything your dog does with the box.

4 Now only click new and different activities.

5 Move on to "shaping" an activity. Pick something your dog has been doing with the box, and try to extend or slightly change the behavior.

6 If the dog lifts the box, try to shape "carry the box." To do this, click him for mouthing the box. Usually he'll pick one spot to grab the box. Click him for any grab that moves the box, then for holding it longer and moving it more, then for any moves that lift the box. If he lifts and carries or drags it, click and give him a jackpot (several treats tossed at once).

7 Once your dog can carry the box, you can extend this behavior to carrying the paper, putting his toys in the box, etc.

8 In addition to this you can shape all kinds of fun activities, such as "get in the box and stay there" or "tip the box over on yourself." Have fun and don't be afraid to experiment!

C) *Murphy has learned that when he offers a behavior he will be clicked for it. He is now showing great enthusiasm for the new game.*

D) *A leap on the box deserves a click…*

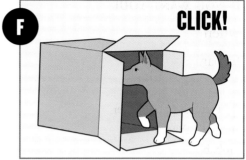

E) *...and so does a leap off!*

F) *Now Murphy is trying something new—going inside the box. He will be clicked for this.*

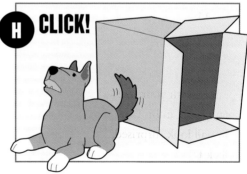

G) *Encouraged by his success, Murphy goes further into the box.*

H) *This exercise teaches dogs to be inventive. Murphy knows he will only be clicked for offering a new behavior, so now he tries a down by the box. Click! That's a great way to end a training session.*

IF YOU WANT YOUR DOG TO BARK ON COMMAND OR STOP BARKING when he gets into a frenzy, this trick is a must. You can teach your dog to bark or stop barking on cue with a few simple clicks.

1 Get out your clicker and treats. You can probably trigger barking by knocking on the door or table. Or have a friend ring the doorbell. While the dog is barking, click and immediately give him a treat.

2 As he swallows the treat, make a "Shh" gesture with your free hand, right in his face. He will look surprised. Click that expression, move your hand away and treat.

A) *When Murphy begins barking his owner immediately clicks and gives him a treat.*

3 Wait for the barking to start again (or trigger it). Click during the bark, and treat. As the dog swallows, surprise him again with the "Shh" cue, click and treat. Repeat the sequence several times.

4 As the "Shh" cue starts to work, you'll see your dog try to keep his mouth closed, after he's eaten the treat for barking. He wants to earn that next click and treat. Great!

5 Now say "Speak!" and click the next bark. Follow with the "Shh" cue instead of the treat, and then click and treat for silence. You are teaching two cues. As he is learning the "Speak" cue he may whine or yip. Click any sound at first, then just "woof."

B) *While Murphy is chewing and swallowing the treat (and is therefore not barking), his owner gets close to his face and makes a "Shh" gesture. Soon he will learn the verbal cues to bark and stop barking.*

6 To make the new cues very permanent, keep clicker and treats handy and reinforce "Speak" and "Shh" at least once or twice any time he barks, for a few days.

7 Now you will be able to use the "Speak" cue by itself for a cute trick and the "Shh" gesture by itself anytime to stop nuisance barking.

Find the Keys

THIS IS A FUN GAME TO PLAY WITH YOUR PET, AND CAN END UP TO BE quite useful. You can train your dog to find lost items using the clicker!

1 Go into a quiet room with your clicker, treats, dog, and keys.

2 Rub a treat on the keys and hold them out to your dog. Click and treat when she sniffs. Repeat several times.

3 Hold the keys and wait. Let your dog nose and bump them. Click and treat for harder bumps.

4 Let your dog see you tuck the keys partway under a pillow. Click and treat when your dog bumps them with her nose.

5 Next, begin putting the keys out of sight—under a pillow, under the edge of the couch, or on a chair. (You may want to have someone else distract your dog while you do this.)

A) *Murphy's owner has rubbed a treat on his keys and holds them near Murphy so he will sniff them. When that happens he will get a click and a treat.*

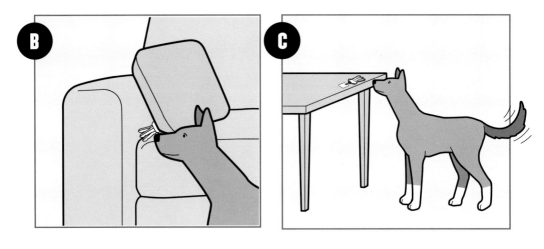

B) *The keys have been placed under a pillow while Murphy watched and now Murphy noses them and gets a click and treat.*

C) *This time the keys have been placed on a high table while Murphy was not looking, but he has learned the trick and cue and can find them easily.*

6 Click and treat when your dog searches for the keys with her nose. Repeat several times.

7 Now say, "Find the keys" at the start of each new search.

8 Make the keys harder to find. Put them on a table or other higher location. (Don't click the dog for jumping! Let her point towards the keys with her nose.) Click if she finds them and wags her tail.

9 Now try hiding the keys in one room, and starting the search in another. Say, "Find the keys!"

10 Next time you can't find your keys, ask your dog to find them. She'll know where they are!

Fetch

A CLASSIC DOG AND OWNER GAME, FETCH IS A GOOD TIME FOR BOTH you and your dog. Teach your dog to fetch everything from a stick to the newspaper using your clicker.

1 Sit in a quiet room with your dog, a clicker, and TWO identical throwing items: toys, sticks, or balls.

2 Tease your dog with a toy until she grabs it in her mouth. It's ok if she runs away with it. When she looks at you again, hold up the OTHER toy. If she loosens her grip, click and hold out the new toy.

3 Wiggle the new toy to try and make it tempting. Let her grab the toy in your hand while you pick up the first toy.

4 Now hold up the toy you have. When she drops the toy she has, click, and make her reach or jump for the toy you have. Let her take it.

A) *Murphy has one toy in his mouth while his owner teases him with another toy in her hand. Murphy will drop his toy to get the other toy.*

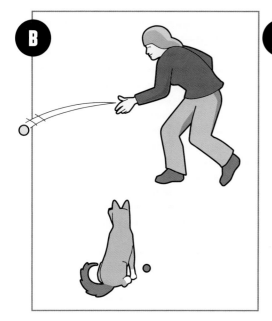

FETCH!

B) *This time Murphy's owner throws the toy she has when Murphy drops his toy.*

C) *Murphy's owner has discarded the second toy and now Murphy listens to the "Fetch" cue as he goes after the thrown toy so he can return it to his owner for another throw.*

5   Call her. When she is coming in your direction, even if she is not very close, click and hold up your toy. When she drops the toy she has, click and toss your toy. Retrieve the toy she dropped and repeat.

6   Next, call her back to you. When she gets closer, hold up your toy. When she drops the toy she has, click and throw the other one past her (so that she has to run out to get it). Repeat.

7 When she starts dropping the toy near your feet, pick up her toy, click, and throw it. Now you can omit the second toy.

8 Watch out for signs of fatigue. If you get this far in one session you are doing great! Put the toys away, click and give a special treat.

9 Play in different rooms and outdoors. When your dog understands that by returning the toy to you she can get you to throw it again, she will no longer play keep-away.

Hide and Seek

THIS IS A GREAT GAME TO PLAY WITH YOUR DOG—IT'S FUN FOR owners and pets. You hide and your dog gets a click and treat when he finds you!

1 Start by standing in an open doorway, near your dog. Call your dog, and click and treat.

2 Move to another part of the room; call the dog and when he looks at you, click and treat.

3 Open a closet door, stand between the door and the wall, and call to your dog. When you see his face, click and treat. Move to the other side of the door. Repeat.

4 Stand in the closet with the door slightly ajar. Call your dog; click and treat when his nose is in the door.

5 Next, call your dog from another room, and click and treat when he comes.

6 Hide in different spots during the day. Start using a verbal cue, such as "Find me" to call your dog. Click and treat when you're found.

7 Enlist friends or children. Give them a clicker and treats and ask them to hide nearby, in an easy place. Tell the dog to

"Find _____," and go looking together. Let the hiders click and treat when the dog finds them.

8 Take turns hiding. When the dog finds you, click and treat and tell him, "Find _____." Let the dog go looking by himself while you hide again. At this point, hiders stop calling the dog; instead, the person who has been found clicks and treats and then tells your dog to look for the other person.

A) *Murphy's owner stands in an open doorway and calls Murphy. When Murphy comes near the door, he gets a click and a treat.*

B) *Next his owner stands in a closet with the door ajar. When Murphy's nose touches the door he gets a click and a treat.*

C **FIND BOBBY!**

C) *Now Murphy can find anyone in the house by name cue. When he finds Bobby he will get a click and treat.*

9 Soon your dog will be able to find anyone by name. Since the hider will always reward with a click and a treat, your dog will love playing!

Shut the Door

THIS CLEVER TRICK WILL NOT ONLY AMAZE YOUR FRIENDS AND FAMILY but may even be useful to you around the house or office. To perform this trick your dog must push a door with his nose until it shuts. Smaller dogs may prefer to close a cabinet or a drawer as an alternative. (By the way, cats can learn this trick too.)

1   Start by teaching your dog to target a sticky note with his nose for a click and treat. Hold a sticky note in the palm of your hand and show it to the dog. Click for showing any interest in it (a look, a sniff, a nose touch). You may rub a treat on the sticky note to give it a tempting smell, if the dog is not interested at first.

2   Once you have your dog interested in the sticky note, be pickier about what you click. You might choose closer or longer sniffing. Then wait for actually touching the nose to the note.

3   When you have deliberate nose touches occurring promptly and repeatedly, it's time to move the note to the door or cabinet. Close the door. Hold the sticky note near the door at first, always in the same area. After several successful touches, clicks,

A) Murphy's owner makes a sticky note into a target by holding it near Murphy's nose. Murphy gets a click and treat for showing interest or touching his nose to it.

and treats, gradually transfer the note to the door and move your hand away. Click and treat two or three nose pokes each time you separate note and hand further. If the dog seems confused or hesitates, reduce the distance between note and your hand a little for one or two touches and clicks. Then widen it again.

B) *Eventually Murphy's owner leaves the sticky note on a closed door for Murphy to approach. When he touches his nose to it he is ready for the next step.*

4 When the dog is firmly nosing the note on the door without looking for your hand, increase the strength of the nose touch. Start off by waiting for two touches before clicking; then alternate between clicking the first touch and clicking the second or third touch. This usually gets the dog to try harder to get the click to happen, which usually means a bigger push.

5 Now open the door (only an inch or so at first) so that you can determine the strength of the touches. Gradually withhold the click for weak touches and click for slightly stronger touches.

6 The next step is to click only those touches that are strong enough to move the door. Start with only slight movement at first. Gradually drop out the weaker moves and click only more forceful movement.

7 One way to speed things up is to give a jackpot—multiple treats or an especially delicious treat—for the touches that actually move the door, and either ignore or give a lesser treat for all other touches. Once the dog starts to understand that the touches that move the door are the ones that really pay off, you can stop clicking any other type of touches.

C) *Now the door is slightly open. When Murphy noses the sticky note target hard enough, he will close the door and get a jackpot!*

8 When the dog is consistently moving the door, watch for pushes that actually close the door. Click and give a jackpot for pushes that are hard enough to make the door shut.

D) *Murphy is now ready to follow a cue. His owner says, "Shut the door" right before he pushes the door shut with his nose. Soon he will be able to follow the cue at anytime!*

SHUT THE
DOOR

9 Add the cue "Shut the door" right before the dog pushes the door shut. Now start the dog from further away, so he has to walk to the door to shut it. Now practice on other doors around the house, or on cupboards or open drawers, until he'll respond to the cue wherever he is.

THIS TRICK REQUIRES THE DOG TO LOOK "SORRY" BY PUTTING HER chin on the ground between her paws. Though soulful eyes are not a trained part of this trick, many dogs develop a wonderfully "sad" look upwards while holding the pose.

1 If your dog already lies down on command, ask your dog to lie down and click and treat when she lands in position. Deliver the treat on the ground right between her front paws. If your dog does not know the "down" cue, start the training when she happens to be lying down anyway.

2 While she is eating her treat, click and treat again, delivering the treat in the same spot on the floor between her paws. Repeat for 10 repetitions.

3 After the 10 repetitions watch and wait. If she dips her head down at all, capture this motion with a click and deliver the treat between her front paws.

A) *When Murphy is lying down his owner puts a treat between his two paws.*

4 Once she is dipping her head on purpose, wait for two or three head dips before you click. Deliver the treat between her paws.

5 Sometimes wait for two head dips before she gets her click, then for three.

6 Wait her out now and only click the head dips that are closer to the ground, until her chin is touching the ground regularly.

7 Wait her out again for multiple chin touches to the floor before you click and treat.

8 Now watch and wait until she leaves her chin on the ground for a split second. Click while her chin is on the ground, and deliver the treat between her paws.

B) *While Murphy eats his treat his owner clicks and gives him another treat. This will teach him to put his head down.*

9 After several repetitions, delay your click yet again until the chin has been on the floor for longer. You can tell by saying the alphabet, "a-b-c-d-e-f-g," to yourself. Did you get to "d" before she moved? Fine. Next time click when you get to "f" or "g," gradually clicking only for longer duration of chin touches.

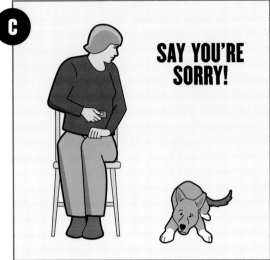

SAY YOU'RE SORRY!

10 Once the dog is offering chin to floor touches with some duration, add the cue "Say you're sorry." Try to time your cue to just before the chin touches the floor.

11 Repeat the cue, the chin-on-floor behavior, clicks, and treats, in other parts of the house and outdoors, until your dog will say "Sorry!" whenever asked.

C) *Now Murphy has learned to respond to the cue "Say you're sorry" and rests his head on the ground while looking up at his owner.*

ADDITIONAL RESOURCES

"The more you learn, the more you'll know;
the more you know, the better you'll be."
—*Morgan Spector, author,*
Clicker Training for Obedience

This book has introduced you to the wonderful world of positive reinforcement and clicker training. But it can't cover everything about clicker training! Now that clicker training for dogs and other animals has spread all over the world, there are many places to learn more and get answers to your questions.

The biggest source of clicker training information is the Internet; and the biggest clicker training site, by far, is www.clickertraining.com. Here you'll find: advice for beginners; in-depth articles for advanced trainers; the Clicker Community area, with special sections such as a clicker events page, an Honor Roll, a "find a trainer" feature, frequent newsletters, and a huge collection of links to related clicker sites including foreign language links. This big Web site also has special sections about clicker training for dogs and specific dog activities, as well as for cats, horses, birds, and small pets. It also features information and links on TAGteaching, the human application of marker-based shaping. New articles and features are added monthly. This site also features an online store selling clickers and clicker-related books, videos, and gear.

Other Online Resources

The site www.clickersolutions.com is beginner-friendly and has a discussion list for owners of dogs and other animals. It is moderated by Melissa Alexander, author of *Click for Joy! Questions and Answers from Clicker Trainers and their Dogs.*

Want to clicker train your cat, your horse, or your bird? Alexandra Kurland, pioneering author of *Clicker Training for Horses* and other books and videos, maintains a website, www.theclickercenter.com, and monitors the very active ClickRyder list. Melinda Johnson, author of *Getting Started: Clicker Training Birds*, moderates the Birdclick Yahoo group and discussion list for bird enthusiasts. Many other clicker groups and lists may be found at www.groups. yahoo.com for clicker training birds, cats, and other pets, and for special interests such as clicker training the hunting dog, teaching clicker training, and clicking with service dogs. Look also in the Clicker Community Resources section at www.clickertraining.com/community for links to lists for zoo training, falconry, and other special interests.

Education Seminars and Events

Whether you are a beginner or a pro, the quickest way to take your clicker training to the next level is to attend ClickerExpo, a three-day, multi-track teaching program held two or three times a year in different U.S. cities. Clicker training experts teach courses ranging from novice to highly advanced across a wide range of subjects and applications. Well-behaved dogs are welcome, and the program includes game nights and special tours. For current information visit www.clickerexpo.com.

Many clicker trainers, including the ClickerExpo faculty, also teach one- and two-day seminars to private groups and organizations. See www. clickertraining.com/events for a calendar of events and information.

Equipment: What You Need and Where to Find It

Clickers are like pens, or safety pins. You need several, because you use them in different places, and you lose them or lend them. Replacement clickers can be found at many pet stores and pet catalogs. Not all clickers are equally useful or well made. The traditional "box" clicker has been a staple of clicker trainers. The newer i-Click that comes with this book is quieter, ergonomically shaped to fit into most hands, and has a raised button to improve your timing and avoid missed clicks. It's also easier for people with physical disabilities to use. A digital Clicker+ offers a choice of sounds and two volumes: useful in public places, for multi-pet households, or in classes, for reinforcing students while they click their dogs!

A treat bag on a belt or snapped to your waist can free up your hands and keep clickers and a good treat supply handy. The treats you use should always be high value, of course, but also tiny so they can be consumed quickly. Fresh treats are best for early stages of new work, but dried treats are fine for maintenance. If you are buying commercial treats, look for those that are pre-formed in tiny pieces, aren't greasy or smelly, don't easily crumble, and are both low calorie per piece and all-natural.

Clicker Books and Videos

Foundation Building   The foundation text for using positive reinforcement is *Don't Shoot the Dog: The New Art of Teaching and Training*, by Karen Pryor. In spite of the name, this is NOT a book about dogs. It's about teaching and training—with positive reinforcement instead of punishment—in daily life and mostly with other people; but there are lots of animal examples too. *Don't Shoot the Dog* is widely used as a college text on operant conditioning, and has been translated into over a dozen languages. It's considered the "bible" on teaching and training with positive reinforcement for trainers worldwide.

The video *Clicker Magic*, by Karen Pryor, is a classic collection of examples of the power of clicker training. The clicker-trained animals range from a fish to a mule, and include many dogs. Each episode teaches us something different about clicker training, while at the same time showing fascinating real-life training results, from overcoming fear to teaching new skills. It is a convincing experience for strangers to clicker training.

Magazines and newsletters are good sources of continuing information. *Teaching Dogs* is an excellent British bimonthly magazine devoted to clicker training. *The Clicker Journal* is a bimonthly newsletter with articles about clicker training.

A new way to help you learn and advance your skills is through an ingenious game called "*You don't say!*"—originally developed by trainer Kay Laurence. The game helps you to learn the skill of clicker training by taking turns learning and teaching other people to arrange and move various small objects without verbal instructions. It's great fun for kids and adults.

Dogs: The Basics If this is your first dog, or if you're new to clicker training, the book *Clicking with Your Dog, Step by Step in Pictures*, by Peggy Tillman, is a big help. It shows you how to click almost a hundred behaviors, from ordinary household manners to tricks and outdoor skills. Each behavior has text on the left-hand page, explaining the behavior and why it's useful, and step-by-step drawings on the right-hand page, showing you when and what to click. Different family members (including children nine-years-old or over) can pick a behavior and each teach the dog something different.

Click! Dog Training System is great for teaching basic obedience skills and comes packaged with a clicker.

If you're full of doubts and questions—or dealing with friends or family members who don't "get it" and are giving you a hard time about clicker training, you need *Click for Joy: Questions and Answers from Clicker Trainers and Their Dogs*, by Melissa Alexander. Compiled from the Clicker Solutions online e-list, this book has helped thousands of people counter arguments about clicker training. "Why can't you just use your voice?" "Won't the dog get fat, with all those treats?" "Will you have to use a clicker forever?" "What do you mean, all positive! What if the dog does something wrong?" The author has pooled the best answers from the contributors to her list, put one question per page, and everthing is cross-referenced, indexed, and bolstered with real-life stories. It is entertaining, sensible, useful, and best of all, irrefutable.

If you have a dog with "issues," such as aggression, fearfulness, or out-of-control barking or jumping up, you'll find Emma Parsons' *Click to Calm: Healing the Aggressive Dog* very useful. This reassuring book offers simple and proven "recipes" for clicker training alternative behaviors, to ease or replace the reactive behavior that can be so distressing. *Click to Calm* includes sound instructions for managing the environment to make things easier for you and the dog, and practical tips for changing your own behavior to avoid triggering or reinforcing the behavior you don't want.

Raising a Puppy, Clicker-Style

Got a new puppy? *Clicker Puppy*, by Canadian trainer Joan Orr, is a delightful introduction to clicker training, featuring all kinds of puppies, from eight weeks to four months—with children as young as nine doing the training. The clicks aren't always perfectly timed, but the puppies learn fast anyway. Here are some great demos of how to use the clicker to teach come, down, sit, and cute tricks—even a really nice retrieve—in just a few minutes. It also shows ingenious clicker solutions for nipping clothes and hands, chasing and ankle biting, jumping up, and other puppy problems. *Puppy Kindergarten*, a video by Corally Burmaster, shows crate training, housebreaking, and other puppy necessities, clicker-style. The video *Puppy Love*, with Karen Pryor and Canadian clicker teacher Caroline Clark,

explains household management and basic puppy education with the clicker, including puppy socialization classes.

For video guides to a whole bunch of clicker-trained tricks, from playing soccer to turning the lights and TV on and off on cue, try the excellent clicker videos by Virginia Broitman and Sherri Lippman, *Take a Bow, Wow!* and *Bow Wow! Take Two*. For training your own service dog, Barabara Handleman's *Clicker Training Your Own Assistance Dog* is a comprehensive DVD set.

Clicking for Performance and Competition

A key source for anyone training dogs for performance is the video *The How of Bow Wow*, by Virginia Broitman and Sherri Lippman. Here you'll find excellent demonstrations of clicker techniques for training long duration behavior, such as stays; for developing total resistance to distraction and disturbances in the surroundings; for using all kinds of reinforcers other than food treats; for chaining multiple behaviors together; and for teaching self-control. This video includes tips on shaping fine-tuned behavior, such as the take, hold, and give, without force or correction; for record keeping and measuring your progress; and for planning your training program efficiently.

Canine Sports

Clicker Training for Obedience, by Morgan Spector, covers novice, open, and utility training, clicker-style, in great detail, with emphasis on fundamentals and how the technology and philosophy of clicker training can improve your scores. Many books written for specific sports such as agility and flyball now contain some clicker training information, even if it is not the primary focus. Look for books that emphasize positive methods rather than control and correction.

Other Animals *Click! Cat Training System* is a great beginner kit for clicker training cats, and comes with a clicker and toy mouse. The *Getting Started* series offers specialized clicker training books for different pets. Titles include *Getting Started: Clicker Training for Cats*, *Getting Started: Clicker Training for Birds*, *Getting Started: Clicker Training for Small Pets*, and *Getting Started: Clicker Training for Horses*. The book *Clicker Training for Your Horse*, by Alexandra Kurland, has started thousands of horse owners on the path to successful training by gentle methods; other Kurland books and videos are also available.

Clicking people! TAGteach

Gymnastics coach Theresa McKeon was among the first to document how a marker signal could help tremendously in teaching precise and complex moves to children. Her pioneering methods spread quickly to dance training and to coaching other sports for children and adults. Applications now include physical therapy, speech and language training, special education, and physical education. For more information, visit www.TAGteach.com.